Getting Creative With

FAB LAB™

Creating With

3D

SCANNERS

KERRY HINTON

rosen publishing's
rosen central®

Published in 2017 by The Rosen Publishing Group, Inc.
29 East 21st Street, New York, NY 10010

Library of Congress Cataloging-in-Publication Data

Names: Hinton, Kerry, author.
Title: Creating with 3D Scanners / Kerry Hinton.
Description: First edition. | New York : Rosen Publishing, 2017. | Series: Getting creative with Fab Lab | Audience: Grades 5 to 8. | Includes bibliographical references and index.
Identifiers: LCCN 2016017296 | ISBN 9781499465020 (library bound)
Subjects: LCSH: Scanning systems—Juvenile literature. | Three-dimensional printing—Juvenile literature. | Technological innovations—Juvenile literature. | Imaging systems—Juvenile literature.
Classification: LCC TK7882.S3 H56 2017 | DDC 621.9/88—dc23
LC record available at https://lccn.loc.gov/2016017296

Manufactured in China

Contents

Introduction

Our world is rapidly changing. Around the globe, people are inventing new things, improving on things that already exist, and sharing their discoveries with the entire planet. We are in a new age of technology—the age of the makers. Eventually, our creativity will be limited only by our imaginations and we will be able to print almost whatever we want, whenever we want.

If the future looks bright, what are our makers making today? More than you might guess—toys, art, guitars, robots, food, and more. This book will explore not only what they make, but also how they make and the tools they use. Computers are crucial to this new way of making things. They allow users to perform tasks that would be too time-consuming or nearly impossible for humans to do without them.

Using computers to make things is called digital fabrication. This method may completely change the future of manufacturing as we know it. For example, instead of ordering a part for a car, we may be able to download a file, print the component, and install it in a few minutes. One day, we may even be able to print bicycles, furniture, or clothing in our own homes!

Computers have been used to make things for many years. So what is changing, and why now? Around the year 2000, 3D printing was little more than a hobby practiced by few that required very expensive equipment. Since then, developments in technology have made 3D scanners, software, and printers both smaller and much more affordable.

Fabrication laboratories (Fab Labs) provide 3D scanners, printers, and other tools for design and creation.

Three-dimensional scanners are a vital part of digital fabrication. They help make 3D computer models than can be adjusted, improved, and printed out. Scanners provide the link between the physical (real) world and the digital (computer) world. At the center of this new galaxy are Fab Labs. These workshops and spaces encourage and allow creative people to make ideas reality.

Who are these creative people? They come from all backgrounds and parts of the world, and their ideas can be as small or as big as they can imagine. Some can change everyday life, but some may have the potential to change the world. If you would like to be one of these creative innovators, then read on.

Chapter ONE

LET'S MAKE (ALMOST) ANYTHING

Fab Lab is an abbreviation for "fabrication laboratory." The term *fabrication* is often used for complicated processes that can involve multiple steps, materials, or machines. Digital fabrication makes very difficult tasks easier and more precise. It also can make many tasks much less time-consuming than if performed by humans.

Fab Labs represent a new direction in the science of making things. Until their existence, the average person would never have been able to walk into a professional manufacturing facility and use expensive computers and million-dollar machines.

What makes Fab Labs different from other industrial laboratories is the kind of people we can find in them. Fab Labs are not only for people with advanced skills in engineering or computers; the technology has become much easier to use for people who don't have technical backgrounds.

The First Fab Labs

The idea for the Fab Lab was born in 2001 at the Massachusetts Institute of Technology (MIT) in Cambridge, Massachusetts. The Center for Bits and Atoms (CBA) opened with the purpose of investigating the overlap between computer science and physical science. CBA had a large facility filled with industrial equipment that could make and measure things as small as atoms or as large as buildings.

In 2003, Professor Neil Gershenfeld, head of CBA, began teaching a class called How to Make (Almost) Anything. His goal

Director Neil Gershenfeld meets with a PhD student in her workspace at MIT's Center for Bits and Atoms. Fab Labs can require up to 2,000 square feet (186 square meters) to fit both people and fabrication equipment.

was to give technical students a chance to see and learn about industrial fabricating equipment. Many of the students in that first class lacked key computer or technology skills, but as the class went on, they found that these machines could help them in their own fields.

Many interesting things were made in that first year. One student modified a bicycle so that it could also charge batteries.

A volunteer works with a Shopzbot CNC machine at the South End Technology Center at Tent City, the very first Fab Lab to open outside of MIT's campus in 2003.

Another made a dress with pointy spines that could be raised for protection if someone got too close to its wearer. Beginning with this small-scale creative outburst, the focus of CBA began to change.

With a grant from the National Science Foundation, Gershenfeld and his associates were able to open the very first Fab Lab in 2003. The South End Technology Center (SETC) in Boston, Massachusetts, contained about $70,000 worth of fabricating machines, computers, and electronics. The machines and computers were able to speak to one another with CBA-developed software.

The lab's location in a lower-income neighborhood allowed children with minimal exposure to technology to make and create from their own imaginations. The next year, CBA opened another Fab Lab in Ghana, in Africa, with the assistance of the nearby Ghanaian community in Boston.

After the first two successes, the model spread quickly. As of 2016, there are more than one hundred Fab Labs in the United States and Canada, and almost six hundred worldwide. Fab Labs are extremely collaborative: they can share equipment lists, 3D designs, and even people.

What's Inside a Fab Lab?

Think of a fully stocked kitchen. It's dinnertime. Your goal is to create a great meal for your guests. What equipment would you use? A microwave? Stove? Knife? You would most likely use a few items in the kitchen. A knife is important to cut chicken, but without a stove, the chicken would be served raw. A variety of tools are needed to make your meal.

HOW DOES A FACILITY QUALIFY AS A FAB LAB?

Fab Foundation gives four requirements:

1. **Public access is essential.** Fab Labs are meant to be a source of knowledge in the community and must be open for free at least part of the week.
2. **Support and subscribe to the Fab Charter.** The Fab Charter is the foundation of all Fab Labs. It is a list of goals and principles that must be met in order to share knowledge as part of the global network.
3. **A common set of tools and processes.** Fab Labs operate across oceans and borders. Processes, codes, and capabilities must all be shared. If someone makes a bicycle bell at Fab Lab Château-Thierry in France, someone at Fab Lab Adelaide in Australia should be able to make that same bell using the original files and documentation.
4. **Participation in the global Fab Lab network.** Fab Labs are not meant to be isolated spaces. Fab Labs can participate with each other through videoconferencing, attending the annual Fab Meeting, or collaborating with other labs.

Compare a Fab Lab to that kitchen. Each piece of equipment would be used in a similar way. A 3D printer can produce a finished item, but it is by no means the most important piece of equipment in a workspace. Every item in a Fab Lab is carefully chosen and together they all combine to meet the real objective, which is always *making*.

There are two types of digital fabrication: subtractive and additive. Each one uses a different set of tools, but multiple machines can be used for a single project.

Subtractive Fabrication

Subtractive fabrication is building by removal. A block of material is drilled, cut, or smoothed until the desired shape is achieved. A few of the more common tools are:

Laser cutters Laser cutters cut patterns and shapes into wood, felt, and plastic. The speed and strength of the laser can be raised or lowered, which determines the depth of a cut for a particular substance. Some two-dimensional parts can be punched out and snapped together (or press-fit) into three-dimensional objects.

CNC (computer numerical control) routers These cutting machines use different cutting heads to cut hard substances, including wood, aluminum, plastic, and steel.

CNC vinyl cutters A vinyl cutter is similar to a printer but uses a cutting blade instead of a printing head and thin sheets of vinyl or cardboard instead of paper. These cutters can make letters, shapes, and most professional signs.

CNC desktop milling machines These smaller machines perform some of the same tasks as CNC routers. They are very useful in making circuit boards, which are the heart of almost all electronics.

Every Fab Lab is equipped with a common set of tools and principles. Milling machines can cut intricate patterns in minutes that would take a craftsman hours or days to complete.

Many Fab Labs also have large milling machines that can produce furniture and other large items.

Additive Fabrication

Additive fabrication, or 3D printing, is building something from the ground up. It's usually faster than subtractive fabrication. Instead of cutting or drilling, 3D printers make things by placing hundreds or thousands of layers of a substance (usually plastic or powdered metal) on top of each other. Additive fabrication is often easier and faster than subtractive fabrication for making complicated items such as gears and other machine parts.

Making complex and odd-shaped items in layers also requires less setup and equipment switching than machine tools do. The main tools for 3D printing you would find in a Fab Lab include:

3D scanner The bridge between the digital world and the physical world, 3D scanners enable creators to examine and adjust an item before it's printed. They will be covered in depth in the next chapter.

3D printer There are a few different ways to print an object. Most 3D printers found in Fab Labs are desktop printers, so the size of what can be made is limited. Many professional artists, designers, engineers, and chefs use desktop 3D printers in their

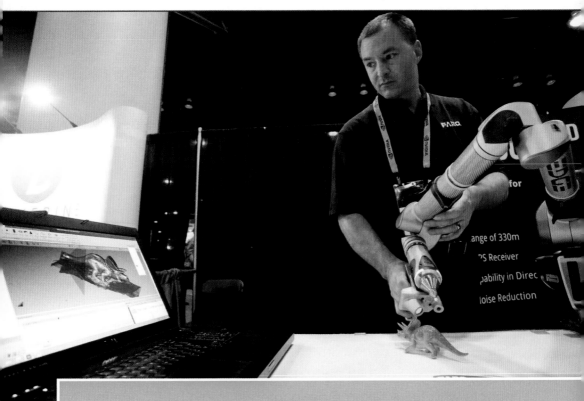

for

ange of 330m

ꓛS Receiver

ꓒability in Direc

loise Reduction

Makers can take physical objects, such as this toy triceratops, and convert them into digital models using 3D scanners. This requires obtaining data from every side and contour of an object.

work. These printers receive their instructions from a 3D-modeling program, which allows a 3D design to be broken down into parts and printed layer by layer. Instead of ink, many 3D printers use filament made of plastic or another material that is heated and used to build layer by layer. Filament comes on a spool and is automatically unwound as a printer makes an item.

Fab Labs also contain thousands of small electronic components (diodes, transistors, etc.) that can be attached to circuit boards (which we can print in a Fab Lab). Circuit boards allow electronic devices to communicate with other devices and are necessary to operate everything from computers to televisions to cell phones.

What's in a Name?

If you perform an internet search for "Fab Labs," you may notice that there are other names that are used for similar facilities: hackerspaces, MakerSpaces, TechShops. Which one do you want to visit? Are there differences between them? Although the term "Fab Lab" originated at MIT, there are many digital fabrication labs and facilities that are not active participants in the Fab Lab network.

Take the term "hackerspace," for one. "Hacking" used to be designated to the world of computer programmers working on code for hours or days at a time. But since then, the language has begun to change. There are websites with instructions on how to hack furniture and electronic equipment. The definition has become broader as time has passed.

The original Fab Lab community is just one of many groups of people who have taken a deep interest in digital fabrication. No matter the name, the keys to the success of many of these

THE ORIGINAL MOBILE FAB LAB

In 2007, the first Mobile Fab Lab took the equipment and resources of a Fab Lab to the highways of the United States. It was built by the Center for Bits and Atoms at MIT and decorated with one of the most DIY art forms: graffiti. Initially, it travelled around the country to increase awareness of both Fab Labs and Mobile Fab Labs as workshops for innovation and creativity.

The lab is a 32-foot-long (10-meter) trailer that contains much of the same equipment you would expect to see in a regular Fab Lab, including computers, core equipment such as a scanner, printer, and CNC milling machines.

The traveling workshop made its first appearance in Chicago in 2007 at the International Fab Lab Forum and Symposium on Digital Fabrication. It continued to travel the country, educating people on digital fabrication and community projects. In 2014, the lab made an appearance at the White House Maker Faire hosted by President Obama.

Today, there are more than eight Mobile Fab Labs in operation worldwide. Theses days, they are mostly used to help people build new Fab Labs or loaned for long-term work on large community projects.

facilities are community and collaboration. Some of these other workspaces may not have the exact same equipment as original Fab Labs, but they all have the same goal of digital fabrication. Some may be stand-alone and not set up for lab-to-lab sharing, but they still have plenty of makers to ask for advice.

Another difference among these workspaces is cost. Some Makerspaces do not get large amounts of funding from the government or other agencies. They rely on membership to keep their spaces open, so there is a chance you may have to pay for access to the training and equipment available at some of these facilities.

3D-SCANNING BASICS

To understand the uses of 3D printing, we should first make sure we're familiar with the basic science behind digital fabrication.

What Does a 3D Scanner Do?

If you've ever copied or scanned a document, the image is flat. What if you placed an action figure on a scanner? The resulting image would still be flat, no matter how clear the image was. A picture or photograph of an action figure is two-dimensional, while the real toy, which we can touch and feel is three-dimensional. The difference is the added third dimension of depth.

A 3D scanner takes a digital three-dimensional picture of a real object and converts it into a computer image or model; this process is called 3D modeling. Once a scan is complete, the data can be saved. Using computer-aided design (CAD) software, these models can be examined and adjusted before they are sent to a 3D printer.

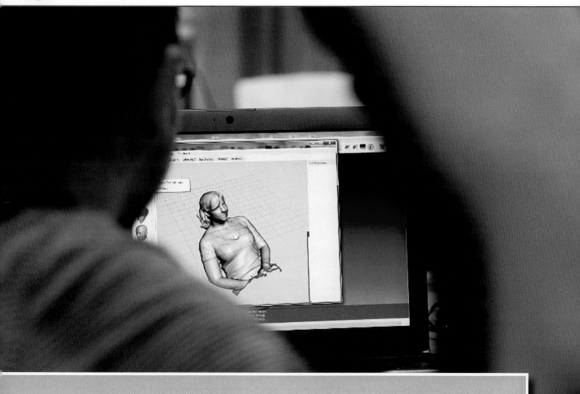

Digital models obtained from 3D scans allow designers and makers to manipulate and change prototypes much more quickly.

Instead of taking just one picture, as a camera would, 3D scanners take anywhere from dozens to millions of pictures, or measurements, of an object. Remember, we need to capture every angle of an object in order to get the best 3D object from our printer. Most of the scanners found in Fab Labs, Makerspaces, or our homes use lasers, although 3D scans can also be taken with lights or X-rays.

Specialized software analyzes all of the data and information from these measurements and processes them, creating a *point cloud*: all of the collected data that makes up the shape of a scanned object. Point clouds are not always printable and may have to be converted into another format for editing. All of the points that make up the cloud are then connected with triangles or other geometric shapes. This is called meshing.

Three-dimensional shapes can be modified with CAD software. Some software is commercial and requires purchase or a yearly subscription; others are free and open source, like Tinkercad. CAD programs allow you to tinker with your design and experiment with shapes and textures. They can convert 3D scans into G-code, a language used to control CNC tools. This software allows users to download a 3D design that someone else created and customize it for their own purposes.

Users should make sure their designs are smooth, with no holes or gaps between the shapes made by connecting the dots.

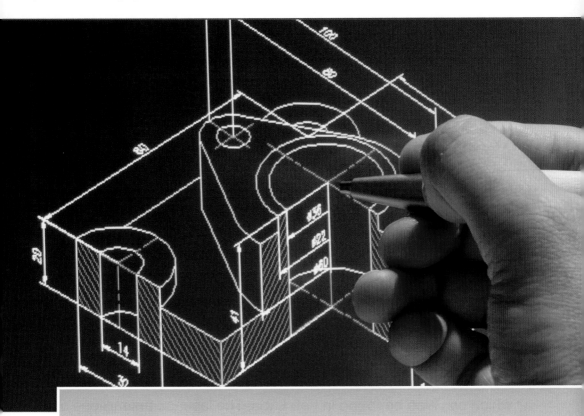

Computer Aided Design (CAD) software allows makers to quickly design and edit digital models.

Not every 3D design will be able to exist in the real world. There may be design flaws that prevent an object from working correctly or remaining stable. Luckily, these flaws will naturally get picked up by a 3D scanner before it's sent to a printer. Catching design errors before an item is made saves time and money.

At this stage, our scan can be saved, commonly as an .stl file type. The term "STL," short for "stereolithography," was created by Chuck Hull, inventor of 3D-layered manufacturing in the early 1980s. Most scanners and printers used for digital fabrication utilize .stl format. We now have a printable file that can be reopened and modified at any time.

Scanner Types

All the 3D-scanning technologies out there can be split into two types: contact and noncontact. Some advanced professional projects may require the use of both contact and noncontact scanning, but the projects in this book all utilize noncontact (laser) scanning.

Contact scanners actually touch the object they measure. They use a probe to lightly make contact with an object in order to measure its dimensions for modeling. These scanners do not have a long range; they work over a short distance. Contact scanning is better for organic (living) things and complicated shapes or machines that need extremely precise measurements in order to work correctly.

In most Fab Labs and Makerspaces, 3D scanning is done with noncontact (laser) scanners. A laser is a very focused beam of light. Lasers that generate heat are used for laser cutters, which can also be found in Fab Labs. The laser scans millions of points to create an image of an object by measuring the distance from the laser to the object. Therefore, the object must stay still in order to get the most accurate measurements.

Some other 3D scanners use LED (light-emitting diode) or white-light scanning. While a laser scanner only moves across an object once during a scan, white-light scanners pass over the object many times, creating a scan by combining all the passes. Some experts predict white- and blue-light scanners will one day be more accurate than laser scanners.

Turntable scanners   These scanners rotate items on a platform to ensure even and precise scanning. Cheaper,

Handheld 3D scanners are used by museums to scan rare artifacts to help build a permanent digital library. Here, a specialist scans the fossilized metatarsal of a sixty-five-million-year-old Tyrannosaurus rex.

entry-level scanners are usually turntable. Some turntable scanners can produce scans that rival those of professional machines.

Handheld scanners These scanners are useful for projects that require more mobility. Users are able to walk around and scan, which is great for capturing larger objects. Some companies have chosen to modify existing technology to advance handheld scanners. In 2015, Microsoft announced that its researchers had begun working on an app allowing an iPhone to work as a 3D scanner. The phone's camera will take multiple pictures from different angles to build a model.

Home video game systems If you have an Xbox One, you can already 3D-scan from the comfort of your own home! With the Kinect add-on, a PC, and the Microsoft 3D-scanning app, you can make and edit full-color scans. The PS4 Eye can make scans as well, but there is a little more hacking involved. A simple internet search will turn up dozens of tutorials.

Scanner Limitations

Although scanner technology has advanced, there are still obstacles that need be overcome to further the technology. Software presents a constant challenge for 3D scanning. One goal for the improvement of digital fabrication is enabling a person with very few technical skills to make something useful for himself, herself, or an entire community.

Scanners have problems capturing objects that are shiny or mirrored. Some very expensive scanners have come close to correcting this, with multiple scans and colored lights, but we are still some time away from an affordable desktop scanner that can rival a professional one, which cost as much as $80,000 in 2016.

3D-PRINTED FOOD

Hungry for dessert? Why not print a cake? It's not impossible. If you have the right printer, you can swap out that plastic filament for some food paste and watch those sweet layers form. Innovations like this have helped bring creativity to kitchens.

There aren't many 3D printers specially designed to print food, but some desktop 3D printers come with different extruders (print heads) for different tasks. Open-source designs for special extruders for printing different types of chocolate and cake batter are available in many 3D printing online repositories. Thanks to computers, bakers and other food professionals can print incredibly complex treats and decorations.

Customized 3D-printed food has only been around since 2012. The technology is very young, but the possibilities have captured the imaginations of food professionals and scientists alike. Even the National Aeronautics and Space Administration (NASA) is exploring the science of 3D food printing; in 2014, they sent the first 3D printer to the International Space Station to explore printing both food and machine parts while almost 250 miles (402 kilometers) above the surface of Earth.

For home use, one of the biggest drawbacks to 3D scanners is price. Scanner prices have gone down from 2006 to 2016, but it is still difficult for many people to own both a 3D scanner and a 3D printer.

3D Scanning Today

With the right scanner, a person can scan almost anything. A few of the interesting uses of 3D scanning include:

Video game designers and motion picture digital effects artists use 3D scanning to create realistic full-body models of characters and actors. Here, a model is being scanned at Milk Studios for MADE Fashion Week.

Movies and Video Games Handheld 3D scanners are commonly found on movie sets. They're used to capture or digitize actors, sets, landscapes, and props. These scans are put into computers and edited for use with special effects. Many video games make 3D scans of actors and use their movements for in-game characters. Eventually, people will be able to use 3D versions of themselves in video games and virtual reality applications.

Rapid Prototyping This is one of the oldest uses of 3D scanning and printing. It's used to make a quick 3D model of an item for testing and examination of size, shape, and other qualities before it will be made in bulk.

Reverse Engineering This allows us to take a complex object and work backwards to see how it works. Once an object is scanned, it can be cut apart with a CAD program and examined. This is very useful if you have one object that you need to reproduce exactly.

Architecture and Construction In 2015, a Chinese construction company scanned and 3D-printed a six-story apartment building from a 20-foot- (6-meters) tall 3D printer. The "ink" was a combination of fiberglass, sand, and concrete.

Handheld or tripod scanners can digitize a building or an entire construction site and turn it into a 3D model that can be constructed by a 3D printer in hours, rather than the days or weeks it would take if it were made by hand. The applications for construction are fascinating. Building materials could be printed to order on site, saving billions of dollars in transportations costs and helping the environment through waste reduction.

Surveying and Scene Documentation   Construction firms, police departments, and insurance companies all use 3D scanning regularly. A quick scan of a building site or the scene of a crime or accident can capture everything in a given moment, which could save evidence and lives.

Replacement Parts and Customization   Some home improvement and hardware stores now offer 3D-printing service to duplicate parts or tools that are no longer being made. The automotive industry also uses 3D printing for prototyping ideas. This saves the time and work of a handmade model or a manufactured one. Eventually, this technology may be used to print complete drones, cars, planes, and other vehicles.

Orthotics   Orthotics are custom-made devices used to treat foot, ankle, knee, and spine problems. Ankle braces and heel inserts, as well as devices that limit movement for healing purposes, are all orthotics. Patients' measurements can be saved and used to create new orthotics; eventually, patients will be able to print their own replacements at home.

Prosthetics These are devices that replace missing limbs or digits. They are very expensive, and 3D printing reduces the cost from thousands of dollars to hundreds. This is life changing for people in the developing world or anyone who can't afford the latest technology.

Chapter THREE

NEW TECHNOLOGIES NEED NEW KNOWLEDGE

We are past the stage of novelty. There is endless proof of what the science of digital technology can do. The next step will be to figure out how best to be a part of it. Think about the personal computer: thirty years ago, not many people had one in their homes. Some people had never touched one, let alone turned one on. The average person probably didn't even know what a computer could do. Now, our society is so familiar with computers that we carry little ones with us everywhere we go. Our cell phones have become more advanced than most of the computers of those early days!

Think of digital fabrication in the same way. Some day, the technology may be as common as the phones in our pockets today. How can you prepare? By learning some of the science and principles behind the technology. Luckily, there are many places to get the knowledge you need.

Where to Go to Get in the Know

Fab Labs offer some of the best places to obtain these skills. The Maker community is extremely supportive and open. Many major cities have Fab Labs and Makerspaces, but you can still get the skills you need even if you don't live very close to one. Since Fab Labs list their inventory, you can learn about any piece of equipment online. Many manufacturers of 3D equipment upload tutorials to help customers, while some offer free community learning sessions via videoconferencing.

Makerspaces and fabrication labs provide both equipment and education for young inventors.

Don't forget about school! Like Fab Labs, your school may have access to resources you cannot find at home. Many companies that make 3D devices have partnerships with schools, making 3D printing possible in the classroom. Ask your parents, teachers, or guidance counselors if your school has any kind of digital fabrication classes or activities.

Since we know that more and more future jobs will probably involve digital fabrication, it makes sense to start learning now in order to grow with the technology. After high school, your knowledge may be able to help you with college admissions and job placement.

Local museums and libraries have become some of the biggest cheerleaders for technology education. Some host hackathons, teach science, and sponsor tech competitions. They also provide another way to learn about the technology that has shaped our history and culture.

STEM: Science, Technology, Engineering, and Math

The focus on STEM is a way of looking at education as we move through the twenty-first century. As important as it is today, science may be even more important in the future. Technology is constantly improving, and innovations have put technologies once found only in factories in the hands of the average person. Having a strong understanding of science and math is going to be more necessary than ever to your success as a maker.

According to the Institute of Electrical and Electronics Engineers (IEEE), thirty-five percent of today's engineering jobs require a familiarity with 3D printing. This number is expected to rise as 3D-printing technology improves. Companies around the world are investing billions of dollars to "improve hardware, software, and printable plastics and other materials." This future planning for every aspect of 3D printing will only increase the need for these skills.

At the White House Science Fair in 2015, President Obama said: "Science is more than a school subject … it is an approach to the world, a critical way to understand and explore and engage with the world, and then have the capacity to change

President Obama inspects a maker's invention at the White House Science Fair. Mohammed Sayed, sixteen, developed a 3D-printed multipurpose arm for his wheelchair that serves as both camera tripod and cup holder.

that world." If you want to change the world, why not be as prepared as you can be? You'll have a much better chance of accomplishing your goal.

One application of STEM is to connect science and math with the creativity and innovation of 3D design and fabrication. In 2016, young people can receive the same knowledge that only college students could twenty years ago. Some colleges already offer degrees in Digital Fabrication, and some day students will be able to take classes like The Art of 3D Baking or The Art of 3D Art.

Many of the subjects you take in school already involve more of these connections than you realize:

Art Art students can scan models, sculptures, or other three-dimensional pieces.

History 3D scans of historical documents, relics of ancient civilizations, or maps can make the past that much more real.

Law In a world where we can make (almost) anything, legal issues are bound to pop up, especially in terms of copyright and ownership. Lawyers will have to understand the technology in order to understand the laws for it.

Geometry 3D scanning and CAD programs can be used to take apart and examine complicated shapes and explain difficult concepts.

Design Although printing a 3D object is the end result of digital fabrication, much of the real work and learning happens during the design phase.

Biology Students can look at 3D scans of plants, animals, or organs to understand them in depth. The "slicing" function of CAD software is well suited for this.

TECH CAMPS

If you'd like to combine learning new things with the fun of summer camp, consider attending a tech camp. These summer programs are a great way to connect with other students who share your interests. Who knows—they may be working on a project in a Fab Lab in another city or country. Most of these programs are for high school students who are preparing for college.

Tech camps cover a wide variety of subjects. Some of these camps are expensive, but many, such as ID Tech (which has camps in more than twenty-five states), offer scholarships to some applicants. Others don't give full scholarships but may provide financial assistance with room and board or travel expenses. While some tech camps are free, these can be more competitive.

Some camps are specifically geared toward certain interests. The Carleton College Summer Academic Programs in Northfield, Minnesota offer a diverse range of programs, including the Summer Computer Science Institute and the Summer Quantitative Reasoning Institute. The Carleton Liberal Arts Experience, a week-long program for African American students and those with an interest in African American culture, includes science courses such as DNA Fingerprinting: The Science of Forensics.

Many companies also give instruction when school's out. Apple Stores run Apple Camps for kids between the ages of eight and twelve. The camp is free and lets students make movies, shoot video, and become more comfortable with computers.

Computer Skills Are key

Computers form the backbone of digital fabrication. Without them, all of this would still be in the planning phase. Understanding computer basics is necessary to working with design programs, as well as other pieces of machinery in the lab.

Try to get comfortable with using design software. Programs like AutoCAD, Adobe Illustrator, and Corel Draw are great for learning design. You can work with 2D and 3D images, and the freedom can really inspire you creatively. Commercial software is expensive, but there are free alternatives in open-source programs

Coding is the language of the future. It drives digital fabrication, providing a better understanding of both computers and the equipment they control.

such as Inkscape. Some may have fewer features, but advanced users can modify the software on their own to add features. These can be shared with others in the online community.

Learning how to code can be very helpful. Check with your local schools and libraries to see if they offer any classes in coding. If not, you may want to consider attending a hackathon. These are coding events that are held for anywhere from a few hours to a few days. Hackers and programmers work in teams to solve a problem or write a program using a certain programming language. Most welcome beginners as well as advanced coders. Again, check with your local library or museum to find one in your area.

If you feel comfortable using computers, you may want to consider building one! Many Fab Labs have access to DIY electronics kits. You can also buy one on your own or share one with a friend. Two examples are Arduino and Raspberry Pi:

Arduino This is an open-source microcomputer. This means it's a tiny computer that can do one job, such as reading the temperature or turning lights on and off. It can be programmed to perform tasks and can even tweet you once the task is complete.

Raspberry Pi These devices are slightly more complicated. Although each model looks like a small part of a computer, each is a fully working computer on which you can install software. With some training, Raspberry Pi can be programmed to control electronic devices and can even join wireless networks. The websites for both of these kits have links to tutorials and other helpful information.

Small and relatively simple computers such as Raspberry Pi can be programmed to perform a wide variety of tasks.

A final advanced skill you will need is patience. Some of these concepts are complicated. They may take some time to master. Building something from the ground up takes a little vision and a lot of patience. Don't be discouraged if an idea doesn't necessarily turn out the way you planned. The world of digital modeling allows plenty of room for making mistakes.

FIVE PROJECTS

The best way to learn about a piece of tech is to examine it and see how it works and what it can actually do.

The projects in this chapter are written for use with the Fuel 3D Scanify (TM) handheld scanner, which is in the inventory of many Fab Labs. It's a user-friendly scanner that lets you start digitizing objects even if you have very basic computer knowledge.

Before you get your model on the screen, most of the work is in opening applications. Support is also available from a "technical guru" (the guy or girl who knows about every piece of tech in the lab) or other makers, should you need it.

All of the steps below still apply if you're using another kind of handheld scanner or a desktop scanner. However, each one is a little different, so be sure to read the manual and specifications for each one.

Equipment Needed

1. **A Personal Computer** with at least 2 GB of RAM and 1 GB of hard disk space. Different editors or CAD programs may have different requirements. Check each one.

SAFETY NOTES

If you're under the age of twelve, ask an adult for help with any of the steps below. Keep aware of your surroundings. The biggest danger you may face while doing these projects may come from other equipment in whatever Fab Lab you're in.

When working with a 3D scanner, be sure not to look directly into the path of a laser scanner or LED. You could damage your eyes. Speaking of your eyes, most Makerspaces have eye wash stations to flush your eyes in case you get something in them that burns or irritates them.

If you decide to print any of these projects, you'll need an adult present. The tools used for 3D fabrication can be extremely dangerous. Laser cutters, drills, and blades are all very dangerous and you'll need to be familiar with the safety rules for each piece of equipment. Safety glasses are always a must. Also, be sure you have a first aid kit nearby in case you need to treat a burn, cut, or eye damage.

2. **3D Scanner** We are using the Fuel 3D Scanify hand-held scanner.
3. **Fuel 3D Studio** or some other scanning software. If your Fab Lab uses a different type or model of scanner, they will have the appropriate software.
4. **USB Cable** This connects the scanner to your computer and allows it to communicate with the scanning software.

The Fuel 3D and other handheld scanners make scanning large objects with small equipment possible.

5. **An Object** You now need something to scan. Consider the limitations of 3D scanners when choosing:

- Avoid scanning objects that are shiny or very reflective. The light that bounces back can make your scan unusable.
- The texture of an object is what a scanner actually maps. The features of an object's surface are like its fingerprint—both unique and textured. Smooth items also make for bad scans.
- Avoid any items that have moving parts that do not lock. Scanning moving objects can ruin the quality of a scan.

● Be aware of your scanner's scan volume. This is the largest single scan you can take. The scan radius of the Scanify is eight inches (twenty centimeters) long and twelve inches (thirty centimeters) wide.

6. **A Location** Picking your spot requires some thought, too. You should have an area set aside for your scan. You'll need to be able to move in a clear path with your scanner for the best resolution. The object should be elevated off the floor to capture the maximum amount of surface. You may want to put a piece of fabric or a towel underneath your object—just make sure it's a different color from your object!

7. **Lighting** The wrong lighting can ruin your scan. Make sure there are no overhead lights shining down on your object or scanning area. They can wash out your scan and make it hard to print. You should also make sure that no lights are pointing directly at your scanner or your object. The light in your scan area should also be constant and unchanging throughout your scan. If not, the scan won't be as accurate as it could be.

8. **Digital Targets** These are sheets of paper that your scanner uses for reference. Since you and the scanner will be moving, the scanner needs a point to refer back to. Without this reference, it's nearly impossible for the scanner to make a 3D model of the object. Attach the target (some are sticky on the back) to your object. Make sure it's parallel to (or, lined up with) the floor.

Okay. Your scene is set. Now connect the scanner to the computer with the USB cable. Open the scanner software. If the scanner is connected, you should see a window that shows whatever your scanner sees.

3D PROSTHETICS IN USE

Jose Delgado Jr. of Elgin, Illinois, was born without a left hand. As a boy, he was fitted with a prosthetic hand that worked with a series of hooks and rubber bands. Working together, they allowed Delgado to open and close the hooks to pick up, grip, and drop items. The prosthesis worked but didn't give Delgado the mobility of a human hand.

In 2011, Delgado upgraded to a myoelectric hand. This allowed him to use his arm muscles to touch electrical sensors that opened and closed his new hand and controlled the fingers. The price was very high, though: $42,000!

Delgado's new hand was a huge improvement for him, but

3D scanning technology has made it quicker, easier, and cheaper to provide prosthetic limbs to people in remote and poorer areas of our planet.

he still had trouble moving some of the fingers. Sometimes the hand took a few minutes to "warm up." After doing some research on 3D printing, Delgado met Jeremy Simon, the founder of the blog *3D Universe*. Simon had built prosthetic hands before, so he understood the concept Delgado was looking for.

Simon used the measurements of Delgado's arm with a 3D design and printed the new hand. It took fourteen hours to print and the materials cost about $50. The design was made by someone else—the perfect example of sharing knowledge to improve lives!

Delgado's new hand is cheaper and lighter. His mobility has improved; he is now able to curl all five fingers on his prosthetic hand and use them to grip and lift things.

If you see a green ring around the target, pull the scanner trigger. You've completed your first scan! Congratulations. A 3D model should appear for you to play with. If it doesn't, retrace your steps or ask an adult for help to see what problems you may have missed.

The Projects

Beginner:

1. Create a 3D Digital Archive.

In the past ten years, many museums around the world have started digital archives of their collections. Making digital copies of artifacts and art is sensible—if a statue or sculpture is damaged or destroyed, its model will still be available. These scans would also allow people to see objects in the archive that they may never have the opportunity to view in person.

What do you have that you consider valuable? Think about archiving your action figures, toy vehicles, or anything that you collect. Your collection doesn't have to be large—it's up to you to decide what to archive.

Intermediate:

1. Scan and Modify a Cell Phone Case.

If you have a cell phone and that cell phone has a case, why not scan it and keep the file to make a new one whenever you'd like?

If there's one thing as common as the cell phone today, it is the cell phone case. Personalizing a cell phone case is a fun and easy project.

2. Scan Something Small and Make It Bigger.

Scan a small object (a model car or anything with a lot of texture). Use the scanning software to scale up your model. The bigger it gets, the more detail you'll be able to see.

Advanced:
1. Scan Yourself.

Why not scan yourself? If you're using a handheld scanner, you'll definitely need a friend or adult to scan you. For this project, find a stool so you can sit still. You could also mount the scanner to a tripod if you prefer.

Attach a paper target just below where you'd like the scan to start. Follow all of the above steps to ensure the best scan. When the target is recognized, take your scan.

Congratulations, you've just taken your first 3D selfie! What next? You can take a screen shot of your model of you and make it your profile picture for your email or any social media sites. You can also export the file and print it out at your nearest Fab Lab. If you take more scans, you can join or "stitch" them together to make a full-size self scan. Make an action figure of yourself and give it as a gift! Save the design, too. For a fee, you can send it to a company that will make a bobblehead or action figure version of you!

2. Design and Remix Your Own Wardrobe.

The global maker community is all about sharing. This applies to all aspects of digital fabrication, including the design stage. Makers who have already scanned items or created 3D designs are usually happy to share their files and information with other makers. In many cases, simpler 3D designs can be the first building block to making a more complex design that the original maker may have never considered.

Thingiverse, 3DVIA, and other similar websites have thousands of 3D designs that you can download to use or remix for your own projects.

If you already have a full-body scan of yourself, why not scan your clothes, too? Just like your body, they have measurements that can be digitized by scanning software. Some stores in Canada and the United States have already opened that offer full-body scans that are used to make tailored and bespoke (one-of-a-kind) clothing.

You can also remix your clothing! Using the scanning software, you can change color, size, texture, and more. Scale the scan down and print out a model, or head to a Fab Lab to print out something you can actually wear.

Note: If an entire object is copyrighted, then scanning it and creating a file without permission infringes upon the object creator's copyright. Trademark law, on the other hand, doesn't apply when items are scanned for purely personal use. You may need to do some investigating before selling your new creations to the public!

FAB LABS AND THE FUTURE

Today, digital fabrication is a $3 billion a year industry. It has made the journey from a tool for toymaking hobbyists to a technology with uses that are limited only by our imaginations.

The first and second industrial revolutions (approximately 1840 to 1914) brought us advances such as the steam engine, steel, and the mass production line. Some believe that the development of 3D printing is a sign of a third industrial revolution. Three-dimensional fabrication is a technology that can both improve the world and allow future generations to truly thrive and enjoy a better standard of living. If we continue to "think globally, fabricate locally," as Professor Neil Gershenfeld says, the technology can spread even more quickly.

Real Projects Today

The worldwide maker community is making change happen in every corner of the globe. In 2014, researchers at California

Institute of Technology (Caltech) designed a tiny camera chip that can fit in a phone and take a 3D scan. Soon, many people may have their own personal scanners as a result.

Some amazing developments are being made by young people who have the desire to help people at home and those far away. A fifteen-year-old girl from California designed and printed a device called a spirometer to test for a lung disease called COPD. The test is reusable and can be connected to a computer monitor. COPD kills millions of people a year but can be treated if it is caught in time.

A group of high school students from the Takoradi Technical Institute Fab Lab work together to produce solar panels for the rural village of Kobina Adorh Krom, located on the western coast of Ghana.

Three-dimensional printing projects can help entire communities. Making tools, parts, and other things on site can save money and provide help more quickly. Field Ready, a nonprofit organization, works with survivors of floods and other disasters through the 3D printing of first aid kits and other medical supplies.

One of the earliest projects taken on by the first Fab Lab was the build-out of the second Fab Lab in Ghana, Africa. It was built with the help of a team of makers from the MIT lab. With less than $30,000, Ghana's Fab Lab was able to fabricate things to improve communication and life in the area. Aside from fabricating solar panels, the lab printed antennas to build a wireless network. This let users of the Fab Lab in Ghana communicate with everyone at Fab Central, in Cambridge, Massachusetts.

Three-dimensional scanning and printing and digital fabrication will be key parts of the worldwide push to pursue renewable energy sources such as those that come from the wind and the sun. Printing solar panels reduces their cost, making them accessible for more homeowners around the world.

Digital fabrication can be used on parts of energy-saving machines. Three-dimensional printers have helped print so much, from electric cars to parts of wind turbines. For now, it takes a lot of energy to power all of the equipment needed for digital fabrication; but some scientists predict that energy will be able to be saved in the future.

A Similar History

Chuck Hull, the man who invented 3D printing in the early 1980s, believes issues that have held the technology back are diminishing.

Charles "Chuck" Hull invented the first 3D printer in 1983. His early contributions to the field have made digital fabrication as we know it achievable. Here, he holds a 3D-printed image of his own likeness.

Progress in digital fabrication has more or less mirrored the progression of computers in our society. In the 1950s, a large mainframe computer could take up an entire floor of a skyscraper. Today, much more powerful personal computers sit on our desks. It took some time, but the tech advanced and became smaller and cheaper as it did.

The world of fabrication has followed a similar path. In the past, factories have always been the primary locations for making things with industrial machines. Today, Fab Labs have taken that tech and made access to it both easier and cheaper. Potentially, home fabricators will become as common and cheap as home computers.

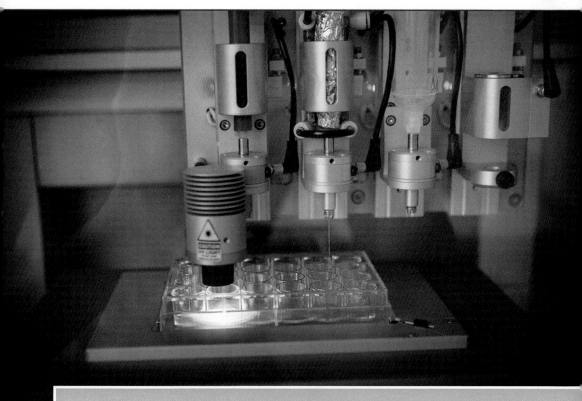

The applications of digital fabrication seem limitless. Today, bioprinting of human tissue and organs is possible.

What's the next step in the evolution of 3D printing? The world of science fiction has often given us clues and ideas about the use of technology in the future. In the Star Trek television series and movies, for example, 3D printing is used on a daily basis. According to Trekkies—the most devoted fans of Star Trek— replicators are essential to life in this fictional universe. They're used primarily as food dispensers.

In 2016, we are still years away from replicators and similar machines but the benefits of this technology could be endless. As 3D technology improves and becomes cheaper and easier to make, the world moves closer to a time when we can all easily create what we need to make our lives better.

4D PRINTING

Did you know there's a fourth dimension? Scientists and researchers have been exploring time, the fourth dimension, for the last few years. What does this mean? In the future, things may be able to put themselves together or rearrange themselves as a situation changes. Imagine a shoe whose laces tighten as needed!

The best-known expert in this new field is Skylar Tibbits, an inventor and computational architect from Philadelphia, Pennsylvania. Since 2013, he has been working with this new technology in the Self-Assembly Lab at MIT.

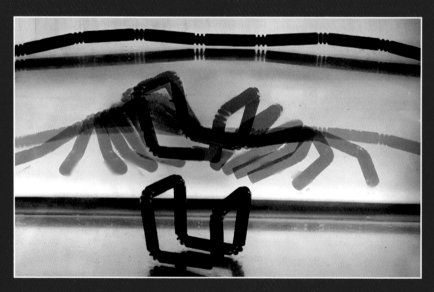

This is what 4D cube printing will look like. Professor Skylar Tibbits is a pioneer of 4D printing, which is inventing objects that can adjust or even construct copies of themselves.

But we are many years away from overcoming all of its limitations, including scale. "To 3D-print a skyscraper," Professor Tibbits says in his TED Talk, "You would first have to build a skyscraper-sized [3D] printer." Researchers don't yet know how these obstacles will be overcome, but most of them believe they will develop the ability in the future.

The Future of Medicine

Many exciting innovations have occurred since 3D printing entered the world of medicine. In 2015, an Australian man was given a 3D-printed jawbone during a transplant. He had a serious bone infection and his jaw had to be removed. Doctors scanned and printed a jawbone out of titanium, a very strong metal that doesn't rust.

Companies like Organovo are working hard to perfect the science of bioprinting—the actual printing of human tissue. The tissues can made with a 3D printer called the Integrated Organ and Printing System (ITOP). ITOP may look like an average 3D printer, but the "ink" is much different—it's made of human cells and a gel to keep the cells together. A scaffold, or frame, is placed in the 3D printer. Then, organs can be built up layer by layer on top of this frame until the printing is complete.

Researchers have also managed to print blood vessels, bone, and muscle tissue. Transplants on animals have been successful, but no one has tried to attach a 3D-printed arm to a person or transplant a 3D-printed human heart. Science this new will continue to be tested for many years before it becomes stable enough for us to use safely.

Starting Your Own "Fab Lab"

Sometimes we have to be creative when it comes to creating. If you live in an area with no access to a Fab Lab or any similar space, you may want to try building your own fabrication station.

According to the Fab Foundation, it takes around $50,000 just to buy the equipment for one Fab Lab. You probably don't have that kind of cash, but why not start small? See if any of your family or friends have any of the tools for digital fabrication. Maybe you could each bring something to the group and build it up as a community.

If you own a 3D scanner or a 3D printer and feel comfortable showing someone else how to use it, this could be your first class! Make sure you have an adult around to help you create safely.

Three-dimensional printing technology has and will continue to change the world. The technology has already brought some amazing changes to the way we work and make. The biggest question for the future of digital making is not if but when.

There are problems to solve before the technology is perfected. The disposal of e-waste (discarded electronic devices), which contain poisonous heavy metals like mercury and lead, is still a big question. Digital fabrication still uses a lot of energy, and the software needs to be easier for beginners before we see the technology shift entirely into our homes.

Innovative makers are hacking these problems as you read this. They could be anyone—scientists in laboratories or students dreaming up new inventions in Fab Labs. One of them could even be you.

Glossary

bit The smallest piece of data contained in a computer.

build volume The largest object a 3D printer can make.

CAD An abbreviation for "computer-aided design." This software can be used to create or change 3D computer models.

data Information that is stored on a computer.

digital Electronic technology that allows the storage and control of data.

digitize To take a physical object and make a digital version of it.

extrude To push out or shape something using force.

fabricate To make an object or thing.

G-code A programming language that controls and sends commands from CAD software to CNC machine tools.

hack To alter or make changes to an existing program, object, or technology.

hackathon A collaborative coding or programming session that can last from a few hours to a few days.

hobbyist A person who pursues an interest as a hobby, rather than as a paid job.

LED Light-emitting diode, a type of white light used in scanning.

machining Using equipment to cut, drill, shape, or grind metal, hard plastics, and other materials.

mesh All of the collected edges, sides, and faces of a 3D object.

milling A type of machine that uses different types of cutting heads for different shapes.

open source Software, hardware, or code that users can use or change for free.

pixel The smallest part of a picture or image.

polygon A geometric shape that has five or more sides.

press-fit A type of part that can be 3D-printed in two dimensions and put together to create a three-dimensional object.

prototype A first or preliminary model of something. A prototype may be used to make copies or can be changed.

rapid prototyping Making 3D models in a short amount of time for troubleshooting.

rendering Using a 2D computer to display a 3D model. Similar to sculpting.

repository A digital archive of downloadable 3D object files.

router A machine that is used to smooth, shape, or cut grooves in a substance.

scanner A piece of equipment that can take measurements and data from a real-world object and turn it into a three-dimensional model.

scan volume The maximum size of a single 3D scan.

sensor An electric device that sends a signal to another device when activated.

stereolithography The process of digital fabrication in layers.

3D modeling Fabricating a mathematical or computer model of an object.

Design Fabrication Zone (DFZ)
Ryerson University
285 Victoria Street
Toronto, Ontario M5B 2K3
Canada
Website: http://www.dfz.ryerson.ca
Email: dfz@ryerson.ca
Phone: (416) 979-5188

The DFZ is a hub for design/fabrication innovation and
entrepreneurship at Ryerson University. It is a collaboration
between the Departments of Interior Design and the
Department of Architectural Science. They also offer free
training in 3D scanning and printing at their 3DFZ
Workshops.

echoFab
355 Peel Street, Suite 111
Montreal H3C
Canada
Website: https://www.fabhub.io/echofab
E-mail: info@echofab.org
Phone: (514) 855-4500

echoFab is the first MIT-accredited Fab Lab in Canada. They
offer workshops, hold events, and offer paid design
services.

Fab Central
Center for Bits and Atoms
20 Ames Street, E15-404

Cambridge, MA 02139
Website: http://fab.cba.mit.edu
Email: fab-info@cba.mit.edu
Phone: (617)253-4651

This is the official Fab Lab website run by the Center for Bits
and Atoms. It includes links to events, classes, as well as an
archive of academic papers on digital fabrication.

Fab Foundation
50 Milk Street, 16th Floor
Boston, MA 02109
Website: http://www.fabfoundation.org
Email: info@fabfoundation.org
Phone: (857) 333-7777

The Fab Foundation is dedicated to bringing digital fabrication
tools and process to people of all ages and helping grow the
international network of Fab Labs.

US Department of Education Office of Career, Technical, and
Adult Education (OCTAE), Division of Academic and
Technical Education
US Department of Education
Office of Career, Technical, and Adult Education
400 Maryland Avenue SW
Washington, DC 20202-7100
Website: http://sites.ed.gov/octae/
Email: octae@ed.gov
Phone: (202) 245-7700

OCTAE is an office of the US government that manages programs and grants that help give young people skills for high-skill, high-wage, or high-demand occupations in the twenty-first century global economy.

United States Fab Lab Network
2320 Renaissance Boulevard
Sturtevant, WI 53177
Website: http://usfln.org
Email: contact@usfln.org
Phone: (262) 898-7430

The USFLN is a network of Fab Labs around the world that shares tech knowledge and expertise on anything from joining a Fab Lab to building one from the ground up.

Websites

Because of the changing nature of internet links, Rosen Publishing has developed an online list of websites related to the subject of this book. This site is updated regularly. Please use this link to access this list: http://www.rosenlinks.com/GCFL/3DS

For Further Reading

Bernier, Samuel N., and Bertier Luyt. *Design for 3D Printing: Scanning, Creating, Editing, Remixing, and Making in Three Dimensions.* Sebastopol, CA: Maker Media, Inc., 2012.

Borenstein, Greg. *Making Things See: 3D Vision with Kinect, Arduino, and MakerBot, 1st ed.* Sebastopol, CA: Maker Media, Inc., 2012.

Cameron, Schrylet, and Carolyn Craig. *STEM Labs for Middle Grades.* Greensboro, NC: Mark Twain Media, 2016.

Cline, Lydia. *3D Printing with Autodesk 123D, TinkerCAD, and MakerBot.* Columbus, OH: McGraw-Hill Education TAB, 2014.

Drums, Brook, James Floyd Kelly, Rick Winscot, John Edgar Park, John Baichtal, Brian Roe, Nick Ernst, Steven Bolin, and Caleb Cotter. *3D Printing Projects: Toys, Bots, Tool, and Vehicles to Print Yourself.* Sebastopol, CA: Maker Media, Inc., 2015.

Editors of MAKE. *Make: Ultimate Guide to 3D Printing.* Sebastopol, CA: Maker Media, Inc., 2012.

Frinkel, Andrew. *50 STEM Labs—Science Experiments for Kids.* Vol. 1. Scotts Valley, CA: CreateSpace Independent Publishing Platform, 2014.

Gershenfeld, Neil. *Fab: The Coming Revolution on Your Desktop—From Personal Computers to Personal Fabrication.* New York, NY: Basic Books, 2008.

Kelly, James Floyd. *3D Modeling and Printing with Tinkercad: Create and Print Your Own 3D Models.* Indianapolis, IN: Que Publishing, 2014.

Kelly, James Floyd. *3D Printing: Build Your Own Printer and Print Your Own 3D Objects.* Indianapolis, IN: Que Publishing, 2013.

Murphy, Maggie. *High-Tech DIY Projects with 3D Printing.* New York, NY: PowerKids Press, 2014.

Norris, Donald. *The Internet of Things: Do-It-Yourself at Home Projects for Arduino, Raspberry Pi and Beaglebone Black.* Columbus, OH: McGraw-Hill Education TAB, 2015.

Ramos, Rick. *STEM Jobs in Sports.* Vero Beach, FL: Rourke Publishing Group, 2014.

Bibliography

Anderson, Chris, *Makers: The New Industrial Revolution.* New York, NY: Crown Business, 2014.

Barnatt, Christopher. *3D Printing*. 2nd ed. Scotts Valley, CA: CreateSpace Independent Publishing Platform, 2014.

Busmen, Isaac, and Anthony Rotolo. *The Book on 3D Printing.* Scotts Valley, CA: CreateSpace Independent Publishing Platform, 2013.

Druin, Allison, and James Hendler. *Robots for Kids: Exploring New Technologies for Learning.* Burlington, MA: Morgan Kauffman, 2000.

Dunn, Katharine. "How to Make (Almost) Anything." *Boston Globe*. January 30, 2005 (http://archive.boston.com/news/globe/ideas/articles/2005/01/30/how_to_make_almost_anything).

"Fab Charter, The." *Fab Foundation.* 2015 (http://www.fabfoundation.org/fab-labs/the-fab-charter).

Housman, Kalani Kirk, and Richard Horne. *3D Printing for Dummies.* Hoboken, NJ: For Dummies, 2014.

"How to Make (Almost) Anything." The Economist. June 9, 2005 (http://www.economist.com/node/4031304).

Noonoo, Stephen. "Dept. of Ed Launches Makerspace Design Challenge with $200,000 in Prizes." *eSchool News.* March 16, 2016 (http://www.eschoolnews.com/2016/03/16/dept-of-ed-launches-makerspace-design-challenge-with-200000-in-prizes).

Ponsford, Matthew, and Nick Glass. "The Night I Invented 3D Printing." *CNN.* February 14, 2014 (http://www.cnn.com/2014/02/13/tech/innovation/the-night-i-invented-3d-printing-chuck-hall).

Rieland, Randy. "Forget the 3D Printer: 4D Printing Could Change Everything." *Smithsonian*. May 16, 2014. (http://www.smithsonianmag.com/innovation/Objects-That-Change-Shape-On-Their-Own-180951449/?no-ist).

Rifkin, Jeremy. *The Third Industrial Revolution: How Lateral Power Is Transforming Energy, the Economy, and the World.* London, England: St. Martin's Griffin, 2013.

Thornburg, David, Norma Thornburg, and Sara Armstrong. *The Invent to Learn Guide to 3D Printing in the Classroom: Recipes for Success.* San Mateo, CA: Constructing Modern Knowledge Press, 2014.

Tibbits, Skylar. "The Emergence of '4D Printing'." *TED.com*. February, 2013. (https://www.ted.com/talks/skylar_tibbits_the_emergence_of_4d_printing?language=en).

Walter-Hermann, Julia, and Corrine Beaching. *FabLab: Of Machines, Makers, and Inventors.* New York, NY: Transcript-Verlag, 2014.

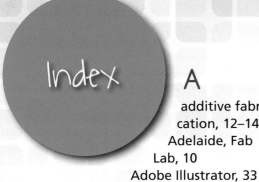

Index

About the Author

Kerry Hinton has been interested in computers and computer-aided design since the summer he won the Golden Disk Award at computer camp. He lives in Hoboken, New Jersey, and attends the World Maker Faire in New York City every year (if he's in town).

Photo Credits

Cover Tinxi/Shutterstock.com; p. 5 Champaign Urbana Community Fab Lab; p. 7 © Ann Hermes/Christian Science Monitor/The Image Works; p. 8 The Boston Globe/Getty Images; p. 12 Rus S/Shutterstock.com; p. 13 © Xinhua/Alamy Stock Photo; p. 18 Photo: Institute of Making 2013; p. 19 Fernando Blanco Calzada/Shutterstock.com; p. 21 Chip Somodevilla/Getty Images; p. 24 Daniel C. Sims/Getty Images; p. 28 The Christian Science Monitor/Getty Images; p. 30 Official White House Photo by Pete Souza/Flickr/https://www.flickr.com/photos/whitehouse/20716691658; p. 33 Hill Street Studios/Blend Images/Getty Images; p. 35 Photofusion/Universal Images Group/Getty Images; p. 38 Creative Tools/Flickr/https://www.flickr.com/photos/creative_tools/14948451470/CC BY 2.0; p. 40 Allen J. Schaben/Los Angeles Times/Getty Images; p. 42 Namart Pieamsuwan/Shutterstock.com; p. 46 Ned Burnell; p. 48 Evan Hurd/Alamy Stock Photo; p. 49 BSIP/Universal Images Group/Getty Images; p. 50 4 D Printing: Self-Assembly Lab, MIT + Stratasys + Autodesk; cover and interior pages background pattern Slanapotam/Shutterstock.com.

Designer: Nicole Russo; Editor: Carolyn DeCarlo;
Photo Researcher: Nicole DiMella